Beginner's Tarot

Kathleen McCormack

Illustrations by
John Woodcock

BARRON'S

All inquiries should be addressed to:
Barron's Educational Series, Inc.
250 Wireless Boulevard
Hauppauge, NY 11788
http://www.barronseduc.com

Library of Congress Catalog Card Number:
00-111787

International Standard Book Number:
0-7641-7442-8

This book was conceived, designed, and produced by
Quarto Publishing plc
The Old Brewery
6 Blundell Street
London N7 9BH

QUAR. TFB

Senior project editor: Nicolette Linton
Art editor: Elizabeth Healey
Text editors: Claire Waite Brown, Pat Farrington
Designer: Tania Field
Illustrator: John Woodcock
Photographer: Rosa Rodrigo
Indexer: Pamela Ellis

Art director: Moira Clinch
Publisher: Piers Spence

Manufactured by Regent Publishing Services Ltd,
Hong Kong
Printed by Leefung-Asco Printers Ltd, China

9 8 7 6 5 4 3 2 1

Contents

The origins of the Tarot are open to speculation, and many theories abound. What is known is that—over centuries—scholars and mystics have used the cards as an aid to divining the future.

The HISTORY *of* TAROT

Tarot cards are the oldest playing cards in Europe. The 56 suit cards, or the Minor Arcana, are thought to be referred to in the manuscript **Renard Le Contrefait**, written in France between 1328 and 1341. Many experts believe the first tarot cards originated in northern Italy some time in the fourteenth century. As the cards have undergone many changes since then, it is interesting to find that modern tarot cards still retain much of the original character of the French **Tarot de Marseilles** cards, which were made from woodblock prints in the mid-fifteenth century.

Many ancient theories abound as to the origination of tarot cards: one suggests that they may have come from India; another presumes the Arabs—who had by 842 A.D. conquered parts of Spain, France, Sicily, and Italy—brought their playing cards with them to Europe. Some scholars believed the Romanies—who claim they originally traveled from Egypt to India—brought the tarot with them when they first entered Europe in 1417. It is interesting to note that in the Romany language the word for a deck of cards is **tar**, which comes from the older word **taru**.

In 1781 the French historian Antoine de Gebelin believed that the word "tarot" was a corruption of the name of the ancient Egyptian god of magic, Thoth. He thought the cards came from an Egyptian temple and possibly depicted, or were used in, a magical initiation rite. Eliphas Levi, an authority on the occult and magic, linked the Major Arcana (the 22 picture cards) with the Hebrew mystical system known as "quabbala" or "cabbala." He also considered the cards to be introduced into Europe by the Romanies.

One thing is known for sure—writing in those days was a rare skill, and a system of memory training evolved consisting of a series of pictorial images arranged in a certain order so that each image, while leading on to the next, was also a stimulus to release the information previously memorized. This practice was condemned as being a direct path to the devil.

Some scholars believe the Romanies brought the tarot with them when they entered Europe in 1417.

The Major and Minor Arcana

The 22 picture cards are known as the Major Arcana, Trumps, or Triumphs, and are thought to denote man's spiritual journey through life, with tests to be faced, obstacles to overcome, prizes to be earned, and lessons to be learned, until success and happiness are achieved. The cards are numbered from 1 to 21, with the Fool, or Jester, unnumbered. Some old packs place this card first in the pack, as 0, while in others he is unnumbered and placed last. The Minor Arcana—consisting of 56 cards divided into the four suits of Cups, Wands, Pentacles, and Swords—is the source of our modern playing card pack that still includes a fool or jester, but is now known to us as the Joker. These cards represent the more mundane, everyday, personal side of the journey through life depicted by the Major Arcana cards.

Tarot cards reveal the deeper states of mind, unspoken desires, inner strength, and self-imposed limitations. In other words, the spiritual and moral progression of a person's journey through life. Using the psychic sense to foretell the future is a big responsibility, so learn to be dispassionate. Accept another's individuality and possible suggestibility. Be constructive and promote positivity—words can be

READING *the* CARDS

dangerous weapons, piercing another's subconscious. Never exaggerate misfortune or restrictions, or minimize the possibility of future success. A seemingly self-destructive course of action may bring self-knowledge and self-fulfillment.

You will be known as "the reader" and the person you read for is known either as "the querent" (the one who asks) or "the sitter." Usually, the querent asks a question that you must answer, but often you will be asked nothing, and must make a general prognosis of the future that can span from one day to five years ahead.

Learning the Meanings

It requires effort to memorize the many meanings of each card, but concentration and practice will enable you to interpret different patterns of cards before weaving them into a sensible, continuous narrative. It is important to remember that there is no literal meaning for any card and, as your psychic or sixth sense develops, you may find that certain cards bring you a personal response that can be proved valid as your prediction comes to pass.

Study one card each night before going to bed and allow your mind to create situations evolving from the different meanings. Until you have a good knowledge of each card's meanings, do not use spreads involving too many cards or you could become confused and lose direction. Beginners often paste labels with the meanings onto the back of the cards and they wrap them in black velvet as protection from outside vibrations.

Choosing the Significator

The Significator is the card that represents the querent. Some readers use the High Priestess or Empress for a woman and the Magician or Emperor for a man, but many use a Minor Arcana court card—a Knave, Knight, King, or Queen. These cards, apart from representing people, carry abstract meanings. Use your judgment when choosing the querent's card as there are many combinations in coloring, but the basic rules are: Pentacles for the fairest of skin, blonde or red hair, and blue or gray eyes; Cups for fair skin, dark or light brown hair, and blue or gray eyes; Wands for light olive skin, brown or black hair, and green, hazel, or brown eyes; and Swords for dark or swarthy skin, dark brown or black hair, and dark eyes. Age lightens hair and skin, so older people are represented by fairer cards. Kings represent men over 35; Knights, men from 21 to 35; Knaves, girls and youths under 21; and Queens represent women over 21.

Preparing to Read

First shuffle the deck, mentally protecting both yourself and the cards with a circle of light (people can mentally challenge you, imposing their energies onto the cards). After shuffling, allow the querent to touch the cards once, cutting them into three packs with their left hand. Before putting the packs back together, turn them over and study the three top cards, for they often give an indication of what's to come. Before reading, clear your mind, close your eyes and say to yourself, "God speaks through me," as you are a channel for the images being sent to you. When you read, study the whole picture, then each individual card. Look at each card in relation to the next, and relate your interpretation to the querent and their question.

Modifying Factors

The cards can be negatively or positively aspected, depending on the surrounding cards. For example, Strength dilutes negative connotations, so a negative card will be positively aspected if Strength sits next to it. Reversed cards with mainly negative meanings are a fairly modern innovation. However, there are enough negative interpretations in the original tarot pack, and reversals are not used by readers who believe a strongly psychic person will never need them.

It takes considerable experience to read a large spread that uses all the cards, so it is better for a beginner to gain proficiency and confidence by using the following smaller spreads.

The SPREADS

These are the Draw, an old Romany method that is used to answer a particular question; the Seven Method, which answers a question or sums up an entire reading; the ancient Bohemian Method, which uses 21 cards and from which originated the modern, more complicated 21-card spread; and the Celtic Cross, an ancient traditional method that can answer a question or foretell future prospects.

The Draw

This spread is a useful one to use to answer a specific question put to you by the querent. Shuffle the pack and ask the querent to cut the cards into three packs with his or her left hand. Study and remember the three top cards, which may indicate the outcome. Reassemble the pack and place the cards face down in a fan shape on the table. Then ask the querent to draw three cards from anywhere in the pack and put them down in order of choice from left to right.

The first card denotes the past.	The second card denotes the present.	The third card denotes the future

If you find that, even after studying the three cards on cutting the pack the first time, there is no clear connection or answer in the first three cards chosen, ask the querent to repeat the process twice more. The nine cards, plus the three cards you initially read, should give the solution.

The Seven Method

This method can either answer a specific question, or you can use it after the other spreads to sum up an entire reading. You will also find it encouraging when you see that your conclusions were correct.

Shuffle the pack and ask the querent to use his or her left hand to cut the cards into three packs. Examine and make a note of the three top cards, which may indicate the outcome. Spread the entire pack on the table face down and ask the querent to pick seven cards at random.

Keeping the cards in the order of choice, lay them from right to left.

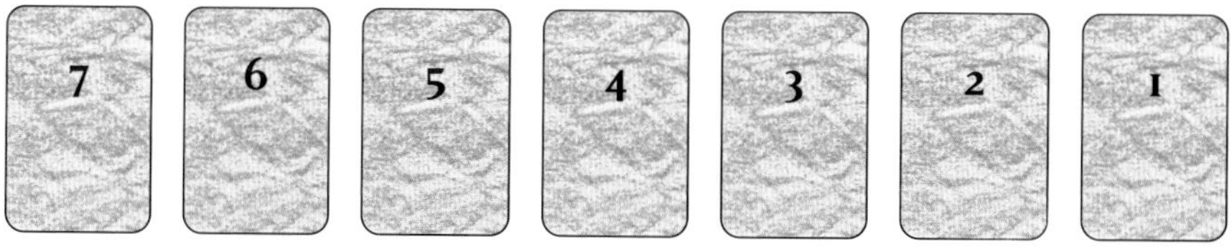

If a question has to be answered, the central card, the **fourth card**, indicates the querent's attitude and reactions to the matter in question.

The **seventh card** denotes the outcome.

The **sixth card** denotes the unexpected or obstacles.

The **fifth card** denotes help, which may be given.

The **third card** is paired off with the fifth card to add clarity to the kind of help (or hindrance, should the cards be unfortunate) that will be given.

The **second card** is paired off with the sixth card to add clarity to the nature of the obstacle or the unexpected.

The **first card** is paired off with the seventh card to add clarity to the influences around the outcome.

The Bohemian Method

A Bohemian spread deals with most of the major aspects of life. Here, each card is influenced slightly by the card beside it and most cards have secondary meanings, so although the strongest meaning usually prevails, sometimes another meaning can predominate. In this spread, more than six Major Arcana cards can mean that the querent is overcontrolled, unable to express emotion, and near to the breaking point. Less than four Major Arcana cards can mean the querent is suffering inner distress, is unable to face problems squarely, and could be living in a land of make believe.

After shuffling the pack, ask the querent to cut the pack into three with the left hand. Note the meaning of the three top cards, then reassemble the pack and spread the cards in a fan across the table. Ask the querent to pick 21 cards from anywhere in the pack. Make sure the cards are kept in the order they are chosen. Deal seven cards in a clockwork direction, until there are seven packs of three cards in the shape of a triangle.

The **first position** denotes domestic matters and close family influences.

The **second** denotes matters concerning self and present desires and activities.

The **third position** denotes matters concerning friendship and romance.

The **fourth position** denotes the ultimate desire or wish of the querent.

The **fifth** denotes the unexpected, which could either help or hinder the fourth card.

The **sixth position** denotes present influences at work or those about to appear.

The **seventh** denotes the elements of luck and good fortune coming to the querent.

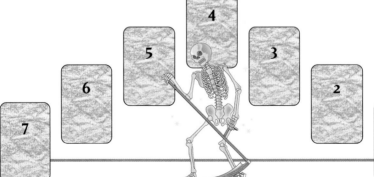

The Celtic Cross

This spread can be used to answer a question or to foretell future prospects. Place the chosen Significator in the center of the table and mentally envelop yourself in light. Shuffle the cards while the querent asks the question, then ask the querent to cut the pack into three. Note the top three cards, then reassemble the pack. Spread the pack face down on the table and ask the querent to pick ten cards at random. Make sure the cards are kept in the order they are chosen.

The **first card**, when laid over the Significator, relates to the querent's principal concerns, or the question.

Lay the **second card** across the first. It denotes future forces or people opposing or supporting the querent.

The **third card**, laid below the Significator, denotes recent factors that affect the matter.

The **fourth card**, laid on the left of the Significator, denotes events in the recent past or influences that are just passing away.

The **fifth card**, laid above the Significator, denotes the possible outcome.

The **sixth card**, laid on the right of the Significator, denotes influences in the future.

The **seventh card**, at the bottom, represents the querent's negative feelings.

The **eighth card** denotes his or her environment and the attitude of family or friends.

The **ninth card** denotes the querent's emotions, hopes, fears, and ideals.

The **tenth card** denotes the outcome.

If the outcome is inconclusive or a court card appears in the tenth position, use the tenth card as the Significator and lay a second spread over the first.

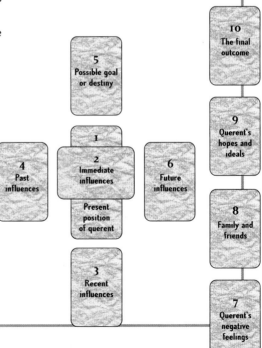

10 The final outcome

5 Possible goal or destiny

9 Querent's hopes and ideals

1

4 Past influences

2 Immediate influences

6 Future influences

Present position of querent

8 Family and friends

3 Recent influences

7 Querent's negative feelings

The FOOL

*An important, strongly spiritual card,
denoting spiritual strength and protection
as man learns lessons and makes choices
on life's journey.*

LE MAT

*The Fool, or Jester,
denotes spiritual
progress, learning
life's lessons, important
choices or changes involving courage and wisdom.
It can also mean risk through recklessness.*

Suggested Reading

1 The querent is trusting, positive, believes in spiritual guidance and even miracles, is independent and courageous, but sometimes reckless.

2 A sudden opportunity could bring a different cycle of life. Much deliberation is needed to ensure you make the right choice.

3 An independent spirit and originality of mind underlies future success, provided care is taken to see both sides of any problem.

4 Success that has already been achieved can be undermined by future carelessness with finances or by laziness.

5 Original and positive thinking coupled with action bring great satisfaction and personal success.

6 A different viewpoint and original methods of tackling problems enable success to be achieved in a surprising and lasting way.

7 Do not be afraid to trust your own inner voice —you know what is right for yourself.

8 Refuse to be swayed by the negativity of those who do not share your viewpoint, and keep your plans to yourself.

9 Listen to your heart—trust yourself, have the courage to start a new life, and happiness will be yours.

10 Spiritual happiness, peace, and successful achievements are the result of the correct decision made.

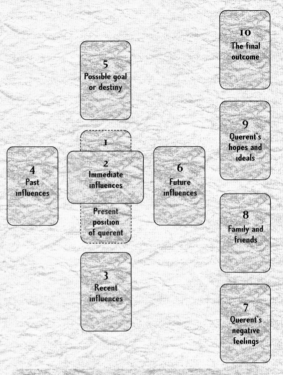

5 Possible goal or destiny

10 The final outcome

1

2 Immediate influences

9 Querent's hopes and ideals

4 Past influences

Present position of querent

6 Future influences

8 Family and friends

3 Recent influences

7 Querent's negative feelings

Cards in Combination

The Fool is a highly spiritual card, and if material cards such as the Wheel or the Devil appear beside it, its meaning is canceled. Coming after the Hermit, a secret will be revealed, but if the Fool comes before the Hermit, a secret will be safe. If the Chariot is next to the Fool, there will be sudden important news, and if the Sun appears next to the Fool, an unexpected triumph brings comfort, order, and joy.

The
MAGICIAN

The commencement card, also denoting duality, the union of personal and divine power, sometimes used deviously for selfish ends.

LE BATELEUR

Look for new beginnings and opportunities that use your talents. This card symbolizes willpower, turning thought into action, and skillful communication. It suggests new skills, but warns of guile and trickery.

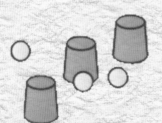

Suggested Reading

1 The querent is a positive, mentally alert person possessing a strong creative talent and excellent communication skills.

2 A difficult but honest decision brings a desired change in life or creative ideas will soon become an exciting reality

3 New self-awareness and self-examination have resulted in the desire for change.

4 A surprising event or the result of a recent project have illustrated talents and capabilities long disregarded or underestimated.

5 Courage, belief in yourself, and positive action bring achievement and triumph in a new, exciting direction.

6 A loving friend gives strong support. Future changes will be successful provided both sides of the issues are studied and accepted.

7 There is no point in wasting time worrying about the risks in a new venture. Act now.

8 Your knowledge and grasp of facts impress others and gain their approval. Just be sure your motivation is honest.

9 Contentment comes from using your spiritual and psychic powers wisely for others.

10 A creative triumph brings a successful new beginning—but true happiness will be yours only if you learn to know yourself.

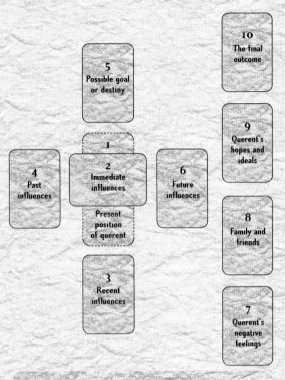

10 The final outcome

5 Possible goal or destiny

9 Querent's hopes and ideals

1

2 Immediate influences

4 Past influences

6 Future influences

Present position of querent

8 Family and friends

3 Recent influences

7 Querent's negative feelings

Cards in Combination

The Magician next to the High Priestess can mean occult power wrongly used. When in fifth or tenth position and Death is opposite, there will be a cancelation of an event. If next to each other, they cancel each other out, and if the Devil or the Wheel appear opposite the Magician, a delay will occur.

The HIGH PRIESTESS

Representing the inner life, spiritual enlightenment, mystery, silence, philosophy, and learning, as well as creative talents and cultural advancement.

LA PAPESSE

The High Priestess denotes inner perception, esoteric knowledge, occult studies, love of learning, spiritual protection, and mystery.

Suggested Reading

1 A strongly creative soul, generous, trusting, independent, and deeply spiritual, with a strong psychic sense often used as intuition.

2 Denotes generous help given by a caring person to develop neglected or unrecognized creative talent or the psychic sense.

3 Symbolic of a new phase of life, learning to have faith in your own abilities and judgment, as well as developing the inner self, and possible occult experiences.

4 Self-confidence has been weakened due to a lack of support from those who have used and abused your friendship.

5 The desire to use your talents and abilities to encourage others will bring both success and deep contentment.

6 Self-knowledge, self-discipline, self-motivation, and positivity bring rewards and self-satisfaction.

7 Listen more to your inner self, act on your own intuition, and remember to keep thoughts and secret plans to yourself; others are not always honest.

8 If you are afraid to commit yourself, you will never enjoy a close and rewarding relationship.

9 Success will be achieved in artistic fields because of your inner commitment and spiritual strength.

10 Lasting happiness comes from both worldly and spiritual triumphs.

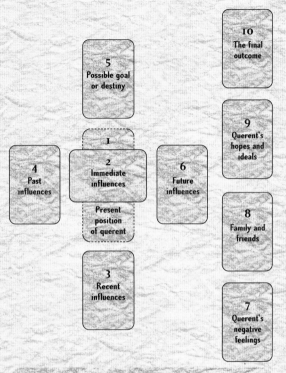

Cards in Combination

When the High Priestess is reversed and followed by Temperance, a problem will seem insurmountable. If it is upright and next to the Wheel of Fortune, there will be victory and recompense after a lawsuit, but if reversed, this combination means insecurity and sudden upheaval.

The EMPRESS

Symbolic of intuitive emotion, spiritual feeling rather than logical thought, artistic inspiration, nature, harmony, abundance, growth, and protective love.

L'IMPÉRATRICE

The Empress signifies femininity, fertility, harmonious growth, both physical and creative, intuition, energy, love, protection, material wealth, and a happy marriage.

Suggested Reading

I The querent is a father or mother figure—intuitive, protective, hard-working, and attracts wealth.

2 Denotes a natural course of events, resulting in wealth and comfort, but requiring patience and strength, or help from a wealthy, protective friend.

3 The beginning of a business partnership or a creative concept with another person that in time brings financial reward.

4 Determination is needed to stop extravagant spending, improve inconsistent efforts, conquer laziness, and eradicate impatience, in order to achieve creative and financial success.

5 Past efforts bring recognition and reward. Past kindnesses will bring help to achieve your goal.

6 Indicates a healing—either physical or emotional—or a reconciliation that will eventually lead to economic success.

7 It is vital to develop the spiritual side of your nature and to understand that there is a difference between love and possession.

8 Remember, real love does not control or criticize, but encourages others to be themselves.

9 Future financial reward, recognition, or business expansion is guaranteed, provided sound financial measures have been taken.

IO The artistic or financial gains you have worked for will appear after a delay with more than was expected.

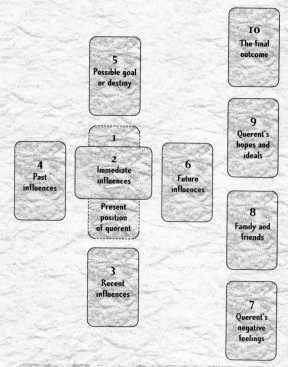

5
Possible goal
or destiny

I

4
Past
influences

2
Immediate
influences

6
Future
influences

Present
position
of querent

3
Recent
influences

10
The final
outcome

9
Querent's
hopes and
ideals

8
Family and
friends

7
Querent's
negative
feelings

Cards in Combination

When the Empress is followed by the Chariot, there will be an important increase in finances. When the Magician follows this card, diplomacy ensures success in a tricky situation. When next to one of the physically strong cards—such as Death, the Tower, or the Devil—or opposite them in the fifth or tenth positions, they are both canceled out.

The EMPEROR

The Emperor represents the dominating male force, temporal power, a governing force, the rule of the people, logical thought, intellectual power, and analysis.

L'EMPEREUR

This card is also symbolic of worldly authority, wealth and power, intellect, passion, romance, knowledge through experience, self-discipline, and creative and mental activity.

Suggested Reading

1 The querent is an authoritative, powerful person possessing dignity and compassion and the desire to help others.

2 Help and advice comes from an older, authoritative, experienced professional person—possibly a government official.

3 Cooperation and help from a government body helps a scheme become an actuality.

4 An established source or an experienced older person helps right a wrong or guide you in the best direction.

5 A new course of action, or a new project or business will bring eventual success. A high position is given official backing.

6 The future will be bright, if you use your own initiative and always take responsibility for your own ideas and mistakes.

7 Do not doubt yourself or lose your sense of adventure. Your courage and kindness will be repaid tenfold.

8 Being strong seems like a punishment when you are burdened by the troubles of others. Learn to say no sometimes.

9 You will achieve success through self-discipline, excellent organization, learning through experience, and honesty in business.

10 Denotes a high position, a new and rewarding business opportunity, or success in a government or official position.

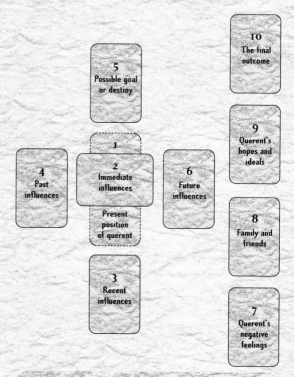

5
Possible goal
or destiny

10
The final
outcome

1

2
Immediate
influences

6
Future
influences

9
Querent's
hopes and
ideals

4
Past
influences

Present
position
of querent

8
Family and
friends

3
Recent
influences

7
Querent's
negative
feelings

Cards in Combination

When the Emperor is surrounded by a number of cards from the suit of Pentacles, an important position will be offered to the querent which deals with finance and brings with it responsibilities and burdensome duties. When followed by the World, it means a loss in conflict or state of truce, sometimes on a personal but usually on a national level. If reversed, the card can mean personal conflict and loss of worldly power and position.

HIEROPHANT

The card of inspirational genius in the performing arts, the Hierophant—sometimes called the Pope—also represents traditional teaching, both practical and oral, and spiritual domination of the masses.

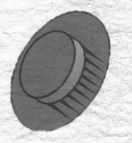

LE PAPE

It can allude to established religions, conventional behavior, a desire for social approval, spirituality, self-honesty, and hidden secrets revealed.

Suggested Reading

I The querent possesses a philosophical attitude to life, is a seeker of truth with religious inclination, and would make a good teacher or counselor.

2 An offer of new work or an opportunity to study that could fulfill old ambitions is about to arrive.

3 Once one's neglected talents or abilities have been recognized, it is never too late to develop them for others' pleasure.

4 It has taken time to learn from experience, but do not live in the past. Try new methods.

5 A new spiritual awareness destroys arrogance and ensures an offer of a future career and advancement.

6 Ambitions are only fulfilled and success won after realistic assessment, efficient organization, hard work, and self-honesty.

7 Do not allow others to undermine your belief in yourself. You have more talent and ability than you realize.

8 We are not all the same. Views and beliefs differ, no one is always right, and there are two sides to everything.

9 Success, self-fulfillment, and happiness will come from a profession or occupation that helps and uplifts other people.

IO A success gained through arrogant and self-serving behavior brings no real reward. Live with the courage of your convictions.

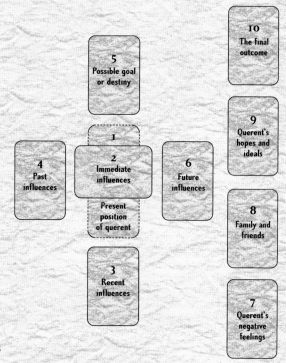

10
The final outcome

5
Possible goal or destiny

9
Querent's hopes and ideals

1

2
Immediate influences

4
Past influences

6
Future influences

Present position of querent

8
Family and friends

3
Recent influences

7
Querent's negative feelings

Cards in Combination

If the Emperor is next to the Hierophant, there will be a struggle between the material and the spiritual. Whichever card comes first will decide the outcome. If the Hierophant is first, either an enterprise will fail or pride will cause a financial loss. If the Emperor is first, lack of learning will cause loss of wealth and position.

The LOVERS

The Lovers card represents the duality of the individual, the weighing up of future actions in the light of good and evil, sacred and profane love, and a moment of choice.

L'AMOUREUX

It represents a difficult choice between an idealistic love and a physical attraction, a complicated moral choice between love and career, intuitive decisions, harmony, friendship, and affection.

Suggested Reading

1 The querent hates hurting others so much that making choices becomes difficult, leading to negativity and indecision.

2 A specific choice, demanding honesty and testing values, and with an extremely serious and important outcome, must be made.

3 Relationships with others make us aware of our own failings and the need for self-control.

4 Time and surprising events will successfully resolve a longstanding emotional problem.

5 Lasting love or friendship based on equality and mutual respect is near.

6 There are two sides to a successful marriage. One supplies what the other lacks.

7 A definite choice must be made to achieve satisfaction. Use your intuition; it will not betray you.

8 Expect a conflict, either between love and career or between creative work and domestic life, requiring a difficult decision.

9 A worrisome problem or situation for which there seems no solution will be resolved by a sudden flash of insight.

10 Accepting honestly both one's failings and virtues, and recognizing the same in others brings the ability to choose wisely and well.

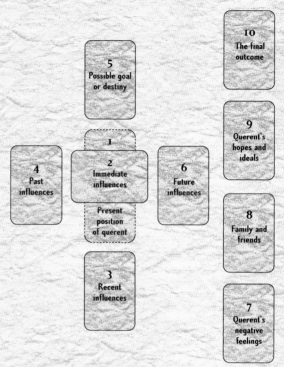

Cards in Combination

The Magician following the Lovers denotes indecision in starting a new venture or artistic work. If reversed in this position, hesitation will result in separation. The Chariot preceding the Lovers denotes a sudden departure that will halt or stop a project, and if the Lovers precedes the Chariot there will be a sudden, shocking discovery of betrayal.

The CHARIOT

The Chariot represents people controlling and mastering animal passions and balancing negative and positive forces to achieve success and triumph.

LE CHARIOT

This card denotes success, prestige, and wealth through sustained effort after a triumph over difficulties or stress. It also signifies patience, endurance, sudden news, and fast travel.

Suggested Reading

1 The querent is strong, industrious, and determined but sometimes overemotional in situations requiring detachment. Can also mean triumphant; a new beginning.

2 News coming, usually through the spoken word, may change the outlook and improve future prospects.

3 Strength and victory result in learning to protect our own concerns from competition, and one's inner psyche from manipulation by others.

4 An unexpected opportunity offered promises a new, exciting project. A new challenge or direction taken brings artistic success.

5 Provided problems are recognized and solved successfully, triumph and reward will come from artistic work.

6 If efforts are consistently sustained, progress will be made that ensures eventual success.

7 The calm after the storm. Significant of psychological or physical healing, peacemaking after a quarrel, or reunion after a separation.

8 Denotes a victory achieved after a series of setbacks or opposition from rivals.

9 Sustained hard work, overcoming obstacles, and solving problems will result in success, wealth, and honors.

10 Recognition and honor will be won. Or an opportunity for fast luxurious travel is connected with career.

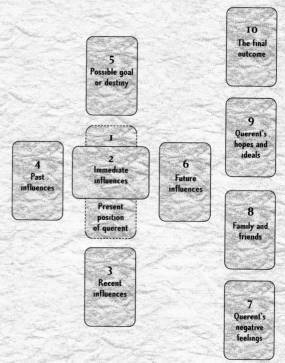

5 Possible goal or destiny

1

2 Immediate influences

Present position of querent

4 Past influences

6 Future influences

3 Recent influences

10 The final outcome

9 Querent's hopes and ideals

8 Family and friends

7 Querent's negative feelings

Cards in Combination

If the Chariot comes before the Moon, something that has been hidden for a long time will come to light. If the Chariot follows the Moon, there will be illness or scandal. If the Moon is reversed the illness or scandal will not be so severe. If before the Tower, sustained effort brings success; if before the Hierophant, there will be a relative triumph; if before the World, ambitions are realized.

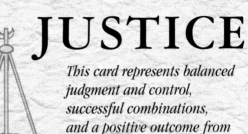

JUSTICE

This card represents balanced judgment and control, successful combinations, and a positive outcome from educational and legal matters.

LA JUSTICE

Denotes balance of personality and mind. A balanced outlook—favorable legal decision, honesty, integrity—the vindication of truth.

Suggested Reading

1 The querent has integrity that will be tested when making a difficult decision. Right will triumph after a courageous confrontation.

2 An authoritative person may give assistance and helpful advice in legal, educational, or official matters that will benefit the querent.

3 Good judgment, self-honesty, and a well-balanced attitude to life result in happy relationships and successful partnerships, in your business or personal life.

4 Signifies the struggle to organize life, bringing order into chaos, eradicating mental confusion by practicing self-discipline, and recognizing our own failings.

5 Making the right decision results in a triumph or brings a legal victory.

6 The querent's moral strength and balanced outlook on life brings reward and many loyal and loving friends.

7 Remember not to judge others by appearance or by your own standards, for this can bring disappointment and disillusionment.

8 What has been given in the past will be repaid a thousandfold from an unexpected source or in a surprising way.

9 The truth will come to light and justice will be served.

10 A victory is achieved with help from a powerful authority figure. Provided mercy is shown, a just outcome will result.

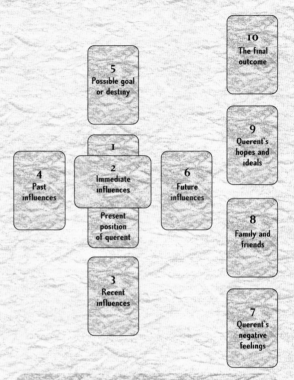

5 Possible goal or destiny

10 The final outcome

9 Querent's hopes and ideals

1

2 Immediate influences

4 Past influences

6 Future influences

Present position of querent

8 Family and friends

3 Recent influences

7 Querent's negative feelings

Cards in Combination

If Justice is followed by the High Priestess, a legal secret may come to light; if coming after the high Priestess, the same facts will be revealed only through legal procedure. If both cards are reversed, a legal event will miscarry or justice will fail. When Justice precedes the Hanged Man, it means that tolerance is needed to soften the judgment.

The HERMIT

The Hermit represents the explorer or traveler in search of wisdom and truth, guided by his own "inner light" and protected by his spiritual strength.

L'HERMITE

The Hermit absorbs some of its meaning from surrounding cards. It denotes inner enlightenment, caution when choosing an unfamiliar but necessary path, delayed achievement, an enlightening journey, and wise counsel. Sudden insight solves problems.

Suggested Reading

1 Trust your own instincts and pursue your own path in life in order to gain happiness and success.

2 If you retain self-honesty and your own spiritual values, you will always be given good advice and loyal support from others.

3 Accept delays positively. Never be anxious or fear the unknown and success will come in time.

4 Clear away negative influences to discover the right road to your true destination.

5 Success and contentment spring from a rewarding progression fueled by self-sufficiency, spiritual strength, good planning, and intuitive thought.

6 The question of the right direction to travel in—in life or career—is answered by a flash of insight.

7 Negativity is conquered by trying new methods, looking at life from a different viewpoint, and so broadening narrow attitudes.

8 Learning to recognize your faults as well as your virtues, and realizing that others have problems as well, gives an understanding of others and brings friends.

9 Trust your own instincts—be guided by your own wisdom, principles, and spiritual beliefs and you will see the way ahead clearly.

10 Despite the trials, delays, conflicts, losses and difficult choices life has brought, you have achieved contentment and success.

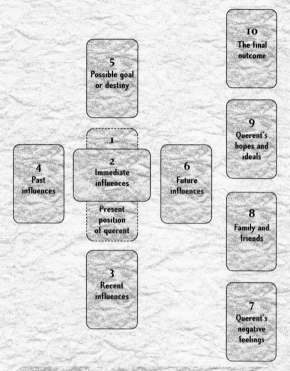

Cards in Combination

If followed by the High Priestess, a secret matter will never come to light, but if the Hermit comes first, patient endeavor will discover a long-held secret. If the Devil comes next to the Hermit, they influence all the cards around them. The Devil preceding the Hermit means his power will be stronger, but if the Hermit comes first, devious matters and dangerous enemies will be revealed by his light, and good will prevail.

WHEEL
of FORTUNE

This card represents the law of retribution, or karma, the gaining of balance and wisdom through evolution, and the sudden capriciousness of fate.

LA ROUE DE FORTUNE

The Wheel of Fortune can indicate a sudden change—usually for the better—sometimes creating difficulties or setbacks that in time could prove beneficial, or could be the results of past efforts.

Suggested Reading

1 Luck comes suddenly to the querent—whether good or bad will depend on previous efforts or methods. You reap what you sow.

2 A sudden change brings benefits or an offer out of the blue brings a great new opportunity or beginning.

3 Signifies a change for the better that could turn everything upside down.

4 Lessons learned through experience bring an acceptance of changes—in life and in people.

5 New opportunities that arise in the future could seem difficult or unsettling, but examine them carefully before refusing.

6 A different way of thinking, different methods, or a different direction in life brings maturity and great happiness.

7 Events have progressed, problems have been solved, lessons learned, and wisdom gained.

8 Imagine a ferris wheel with some people going up and others going down. That's life, so don't let either failure or success unbalance you.

9 Be prepared. Life is about to offer you a new vista, an exciting and challenging prospect bringing a sudden change.

10 A beneficial new life is about to start, or an artistic or creative success is yours, if you grasp the opportunity that is coming.

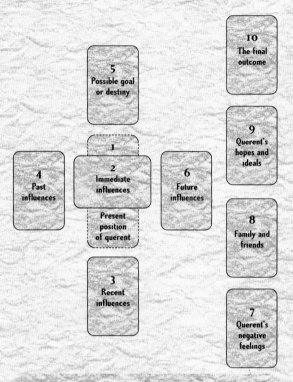

5 Possible goal or destiny

10 The final outcome

9 Querent's hopes and ideals

1

2 Immediate influences

4 Past influences

6 Future influences

Present position of querent

8 Family and friends

3 Recent influences

7 Querent's negative feelings

Cards in Combination

The Hermit next to the Wheel means secrets revealed will bring success. Next to the Chariot, it means a great triumph. Following the Magician, it brings a happy change in profession, dwelling, or direction in life, but if preceding it, the change will take longer. When before the High Priestess, success will come in the arts, science, or literature.

STRENGTH

This, the strongest positive card, represents the moral force of purity, the triumph of the spirit, and the mind's domination over material trials and adversities.

LA FORCE

The Strength card influences the whole reading and has no truly negative meanings. It denotes right as might— courage and power used wisely—love conquering hate, the spiritual conquering the material, as well as a once in a lifetime opportunity that must be taken.

Suggested Reading

1 The querent faces a momentous period or a significant change in his or her life, through creative ability, integrity, and inner strength.

2 Do not hesitate to accept an offer that will change and improve your life in the future and bring happiness, recognition, and reward.

3 Past trials that have been endured courageously have developed inner strength, integrity, and a strongly balanced mentality.

4 Potential undeveloped creative or artistic talents—now discovered and developed—when used will bring pleasure to others and to yourself.

5 Neglected ambitions or plans once considered impossible can put into action through an amazing and unexpected offer.

6 Life changes when self-honesty brings the realization of your own ability and worth, and creative energy is channeled more wisely.

7 One can be too giving, often to people who can drain your energy. Learn to consider yourself more.

8 Remember who you are and the challenges you have faced and overcome them with courage when you are offered a new direction in life.

9 Talent alone does not ensure success, but with your wise use of strength, positive attitude, and determination, it will come.

10 Life will change and improve dramatically through an unexpected event or offer that you mustn't refuse.

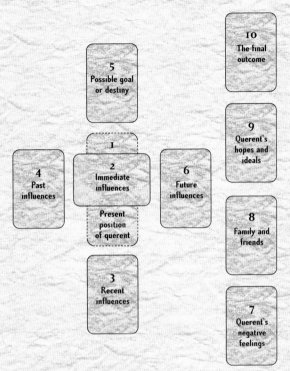

5
Possible goal
or destiny

10
The final
outcome

1

2
Immediate
influences

9
Querent's
hopes and
ideals

4
Past
influences

6
Future
influences

Present
position
of querent

8
Family and
friends

3
Recent
influences

7
Querent's
negative
feelings

Cards in Combination

This card influences the entire spread and is usually positive. However, if it comes before Death it can mean a serious illness, which will not be fatal, and coming after Death it denotes the abrupt breaking of a pattern of life. If Strength comes before the Chariot, it denotes triumph after an enormous sustained effort and when it comes after the Chariot, it means great strength when facing future trials.

The HANGED MAN

The Hanged Man represents a willing sacrifice entailing suffering and loss or hardship, but that can transform your life, and bring inner peace and wisdom.

LE PENDU

This card also reveals a decision bringing spiritual peace, forgiveness bringing peace and wisdom, the reversal of a way of life, occult power, and inner strength.

Suggested Reading

1 The querent is aware of spiritual guidance, has learned lessons, and gained inner strength and foresight through suffering.

2 Symbolic of a period in life when things seem to come to a standstill, or a sacrifice made resulting in a later benefit or reward.

3 There has been or will have to be a sacrifice made that will later bring the recognition of lessons learned and great spiritual growth.

4 A different viewpoint on relationships is needed. A tie must be broken or sacrificed.

5 Contentment and serenity come from a spiritual source, bringing new strengths and beliefs, and a new enjoyment in life.

6 New plans and ambitions may have to be delayed but the right moment for successful action will come in time.

7 Negativity and irresponsibility can undermine security and mar the future.

8 Be aware that others can demand too much of your time and care. A sense of duty can be overdeveloped so be careful.

9 A development of spiritual or prophetic power brings trust in others. Also signifies the ability to forgive the past and deep contentment.

10 Hidden matters, either recent or from the past, will come to light and bring beneficial changes.

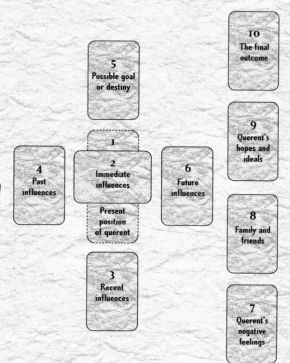

5 Possible goal or destiny

10 The final outcome

9 Querent's hopes and ideals

1

2 Immediate influences

4 Past influences

6 Future influences

Present position of querent

8 Family and friends

3 Recent influences

7 Querent's negative feelings

Cards in Combination

When Temperance sits next to the Hanged Man, there will be hypocrisy or indecision through false promises. With Death, it means a sad ending or a great sacrifice. If the Devil comes after the Hanged Man, a great sacrifice will bring strength and power. If the Devil precedes it, a sacrifice will be made by a marriage partner, but the other partner must be prepared to give more.

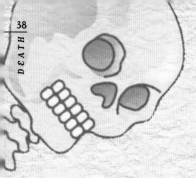

DEATH

A deeply spiritual card, the Death card does not necessarily indicate death, more a sudden overturning of the old life and the soul reborn.

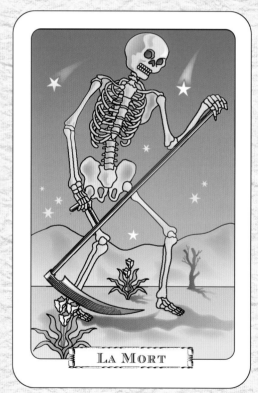

LA MORT

This card expresses change, transformation, regeneration of the soul, shock, and destruction that leads to a new life. It can signify a creative or artistic struggle that ends in triumph and the end of a troublesome period in life.

Suggested Reading

1 The querent will experience a complete change. Past attitudes toward life, old beliefs, entrenched ideas, and views about others will all be altered, leading to a more realistic and satisfying life in the future.

2 An important event will bring great change to the querent.

3 The end of one life or way of thinking and the beginning of another.

4 Face the fact that things change and so do people as they seek to develop and mature.

5 The time has come to stop hesitating and start out on the new road of the life that you want to lead. Have courage—changes can mean great benefits for you.

6 A new view of life brings speedy progress, success, and contentment.

7 Live life to the fullest. A lack of confidence in your own abilities is preventing you from trying something new and of great benefit to you.

8 Something or someone that should have been given up freely or freed from dominance or possession will be removed or will leave.

9 Changes or external events that help to solve or end a difficult situation will bring a transformation of life.

10 The past, with its old habits, security, pretensions, intolerant views, and materialism is gone, while the future—like the sun on the horizon—is rising bright, clear, and golden.

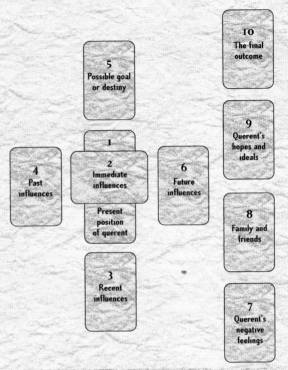

5 Possible goal or destiny

10 The final outcome

9 Querent's hopes and ideals

1

2 Immediate influences

4 Past influences

6 Future influences

Present position of querent

8 Family and friends

3 Recent influences

7 Querent's negative feelings

Cards in Combination

This card refers both to national and personal changes, crises, and disasters. If combined with the Tower, Death denotes a crisis or a calamity, but if the Tower is inverted, it means a narrow escape from an accident or disaster. Only if Death precedes the World does it mean a universal epidemic or world disaster, or even the loss of a national leader. After the Lovers, Death means the end of a romance or marriage.

TEMPERANCE

The Temperance card represents the purification of the soul by spiritual grace, the combining of the active with the passive, and the unifying of both male and female elements.

TEMPÉRANCE

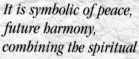

It is symbolic of peace, future harmony, combining the spiritual and the material, moderation, compromise, good sense in financial matters, a balanced attitude to life, vitality, energy, and creative inspiration.

Suggested Reading

I The querent is a well-balanced optimist who sees the best in everyone and everything. He or she knows there are two sides to every story, and could be about to start a new life.

2 A dream is about to come true or a judgment is about to be passed on a matter, either legal or personal, that will end a stalemate.

3 The balancing of the psychic and spiritual senses with the materialistic side of life will bring inner peace and contentment.

4 The cleansing and strengthening of the developing soul teaches one how to live and work harmoniously with others.

5 Artistic triumph will be achieved after a sudden inspiration or an important breakthrough is made.

6 The future will be rewarding and life will be peaceful because self-control has brought moderation in all things.

7 If important relationships are to last, feelings that have been repressed or hidden should be shown constantly.

8 An offer of partnership in business or a proposal of marriage will be made by a wealthy person.

9 Your mental agility, vitality, and the ability to moderate, change, adapt, and manage things skillfully promises certain success.

IO One chapter of life will close and another will open.

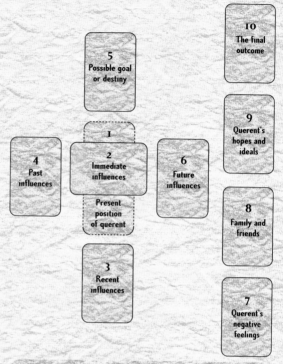

5
Possible goal
or destiny

IO
The final
outcome

9
Querent's
hopes and
ideals

I

4
Past
influences

2
Immediate
influences

6
Future
influences

Present
position
of querent

8
Family and
friends

3
Recent
influences

7
Querent's
negative
feelings

Cards in Combination

If this card comes before Justice, a long legal process is anticipated, resulting in equity and justice, but if Justice comes first there will be delays and possible cancelation. However, if Temperance is inverted near Justice it puts an end to delay and brings success. The Lovers next to Temperance means indecision, but if the Lovers card is inverted, the lover is being deceitful.

The DEVIL

The Devil represents great negative power, negative influences, materialism, physical and carnal desires, upheavals, revolutions, and an inexorable event or change.

LE DIABLE

This card denotes a strong power used negatively, selfishly, or unwisely, caused by fear, ignorance, greed, violence, or superstition; or a life dominated by physical appetite or material gain, as well as a lack of sensitivity. It can signify a sudden inexorable event, either positive or negative according to the surrounding cards.

Suggested Reading

I The querent is warned not to allow excessive physical appetites to sap his or her humanity or considerable creative energy.

2 Symbolic of an unexpected event that cannot be altered, controlled, or influenced and that could be positive or negative.

3 Learning from mistakes is part of life's rich pattern, so a mistaken choice is a lesson that demands self-honesty and self-discipline.

4 The quicker negative influences and habits can be replaced by positive thoughts and actions, the swifter the progress will be.

5 A dangerous relationship or a risky situation will damage future prospects unless you use your considerable courage to free yourself.

6 It is time that you abandoned the mask or false image you have worn as a protection for years and show yourself to the world.

7 Be careful that physical senses don't dominate all aspects of your life and cloud your judgment.

8 This is a warning that extravagance or self-indulgence can cloud judgment.

9 Once you have learned to honestly recognize both your faults and virtues, you will come to accept yourself and understand others.

10 Life will change suddenly. Be sure you are ready to accept whatever is offered and enjoy it.

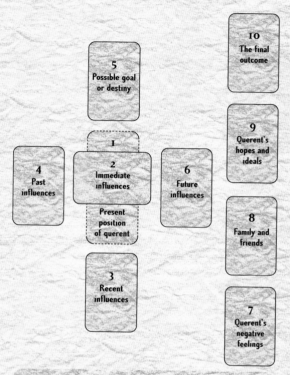

5 — Possible goal or destiny

10 — The final outcome

9 — Querent's hopes and ideals

I

2 — Immediate influences

Present position of querent

4 — Past influences

6 — Future influences

8 — Family and friends

3 — Recent influences

7 — Querent's negative feelings

Cards in Combination

If the Hierophant appears with the Devil, both are negated and the other cards will decide the outcome. If the Devil comes before the Emperor, it denotes a national protest, but if the Emperor comes first it can mean a world leader is threatened with violence. If Justice follows the Devil, a miscarriage of justice will occur, but if Justice comes first, it will prove to be a false accusation.

The TOWER

*The Tower represents sudden catastrophe or change
that brings eventual happiness. It signifies the closing
of the karmic circle, the shattering of illusions,
or a cleansing catharsis.*

LA MAISON DIEU

*Expect a sudden
unexpected shock, loss,
or catastrophe. This card
can also symbolize illusions shattered, selfish ambitions
destroyed, a disruption or change of life pattern—for the
better in the long run— or a flash of inspiration and the
beginning of enlightenment.*

Suggested Reading

1 A sudden loss or disappointment is followed by an equally sudden but beneficial change that will improve the querent's future.

2 A problem that has been ticking like a time bomb is about to explode.

3 Suddenly the old order is changing and yielding place to the new. It is no use fighting the changes. Accept them and life will be easier.

4 Failure could come from unreal aspirations or underdeveloped skills or talents, or the flattery or false promises of others.

5 Happiness and fulfillment are yours if you have the strength and the wisdom to do what is right or take the right course.

6 Take off your rose-colored glasses and see things as they really are, not as you want them to be.

7 A confrontation, shock, or conflict strips away all pretence and brings a realistic acceptance of life, through your own self-honesty and courage.

8 Friends and family members need to know that you love and respect them and appreciate their loyalty and affection.

9 You must accept losses and let things go—no matter how painful— if you wish to be free in spirit, mind, and body.

10 The unexpected shock or blow that is coming which will alter your life will be painful, but later it will both heal and bring you happiness.

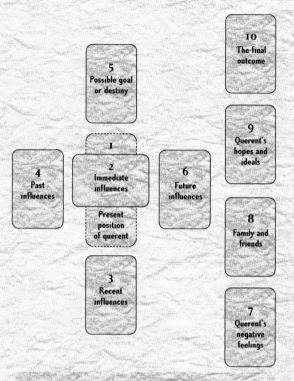

5 Possible goal or destiny

10 The final outcome

9 Querent's hopes and ideals

1

2 Immediate influences

4 Past influences

6 Future influences

Present position of querent

8 Family and friends

3 Recent influences

7 Querent's negative feelings

Cards in Combination

When the Tower comes before the High Priestess, it can spell disaster either in traditional institutions or in the sphere of religion. If these two cards are reversed, it can mean a mental breakdown is coming before a physical collapse. If the World is near these cards, the outcome is more general than personal.

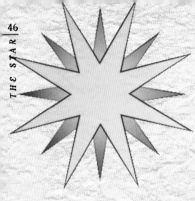

The STAR

This card represents the refreshing of the mind and spirit after a period of darkness—through love, unselfish help, and encouragement—bringing hope and spiritual inspiration.

L'ÉTOILE

The Star denotes optimism, rebirth, spiritual strength and guidance, love of others, good friends, unselfish help given, and inspiration bringing renewed effort.

Suggested Reading

1 The querent is generous, loving, and both creative and practical. A new and worthwhile friendship or romance could be on the way.

2 Problems are resolved by facing them positively, seeing both sides of the question, and using restraint when dealing with others.

3 Faith in oneself, consistent positive thinking fueled by optimism, courage, and energy, will bring future happiness and success.

4 Life's struggles have developed your courage, willpower, and positivity, and have brought you joy, love, peace, and many friends.

5 Success is ensured because of consistent, courageous, confident efforts matched with considerable talent or ability.

6 All energies—mental, physical, emotional, and spiritual—are being renewed to sustain good progress and ensure success.

7 Kill the doubts and fears that others have instilled in you because of their own insecurity or envy. In the past you have suffered from neither.

8 Loved ones will offer help and support. Learning to take as well as give creates harmony and equality.

9 There is a matter that needs you to make a firm decision; this will bring you peace of mind.

10 Despite pain and possible loss, a new direction or decision you are going to make or have taken brings real love, happiness, and peace.

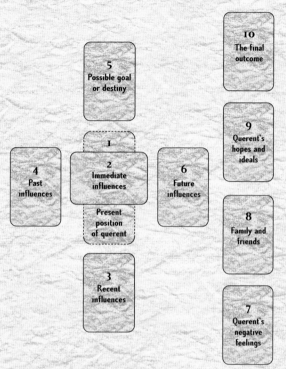

5 Possible goal or destiny

1

2 Immediate influences

Present position of querent

4 Past influences

6 Future influences

3 Recent influences

10 The final outcome

9 Querent's hopes and ideals

8 Family and friends

7 Querent's negative feelings

Cards in Combination

Coming before the Empress, the Star predicts a peaceful, happy and conventional life, and when before the Magician, it means the fortunate start of a business scheme or an artistic venture. Should the Empress come before this card, strong ambition and sustained effort will bring assured success. Should the Devil and the star appear side by side, they cancel each other out.

The MOON

*The Moon signifies the subconscious,
the dream world, imagination, fluctuation,
intuition, occult power, hallucination,
hidden forces, deception, and creativity.*

LA LUNE

*It denotes the
subconscious, dreams,
illusion, mystery, storms weathered, uncertainty,
deception, a loved one's misfortune, or an
emotional crisis.*

Suggested Reading

1 The querent sometimes represses emotions that can suddenly erupt. They have a creative imagination, intuition, and a strong psychic sense.

2 A relationship issue will be resolved by facing facts. A creative venture is about to begin.

3 Be honest about your own motivations regarding a new project, or trust your own intuition in a new relationship, otherwise deception will ensue.

4 Signifies a period of ups and downs and uncertainty in life, during which time you have to learn what you really want and where you want to go.

5 Peace gained after a struggle, stability won after a crisis of faith, or a period of controlling imagination and facing facts brings success.

6 The storm has ended and a clear sky promises sunshine and warmth.

7 Be aware that self-deception is often the product of overdeveloped imaginations. Check that you see things clearly and as they are.

8 The results of past relationships and past actions have taught you many lessons. Do not forget them and make the same mistakes again.

9 The subconscious is fueling the imagination to create a powerful work that will bring both spiritual growth and economic reward.

10 Practicality, discipline, and creative imagination will bring artistic reward.

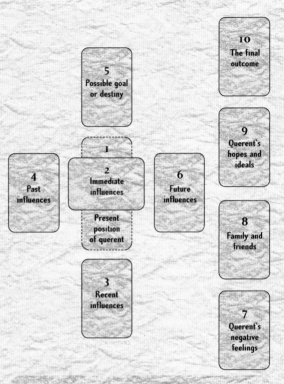

5 Possible goal or destiny

10 The final outcome

9 Querent's hopes and ideals

1

2 Immediate influences

Present position of querent

4 Past influences

6 Future influences

8 Family and friends

3 Recent influences

7 Querent's negative feelings

Cards in Combination

If placed before the Tower, the Moon could mean self-deception, fraud, or deceit will bring misfortune. Justice following The Moon denotes false accusations or slander. If both cards are reversed, the truth will be discovered. When the Lovers follow the Moon, this means the illusion of love, a false lover, or deception and lies destroy a relationship.

The SUN

LE SOLEIL

A positive card, the Sun represents the warmth of a sunny day, innocence, purity, a childlike faith, courage and strength, and joyousness.

This card denotes harmony in relationships, realizing an ambition, successful achievement in any field and against all odds, completed studies, health, energy, material comfort, the end of self-deception, and the gift of gratitude.

Suggested Reading

1 The querent has the strength and the courage to fight and win. He or she can give and receive love gracefully, takes pleasure in simple things, and shows gratitude.

2 A new relationship or friendship brings peace and happiness.

3 What you have accomplished in the past with determination is the foundation for permanent future success.

4 Consistent study or work done well brings personal satisfaction and triumph, or promotion and material reward.

5 A past successful achievement opens a window on the future to reveal lovely prospects.

6 A chance offered for a new career, new studies, a new profession, a new life, or a new relationship must be grabbed with both hands.

7 Stop being unrealistic about what you really want in life. Accept your faults and appreciate your virtues. Happiness lies within you.

8 You have far too much courage and strength to ever give up.

9 A triumph is coming, either from work you have done or because, romantically, the right person is suddenly coming into your life.

10 Hard work and struggle seem unending at present but the future brings joy through personal happiness.

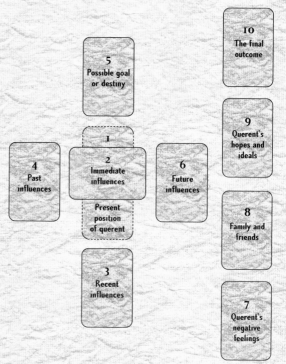

5 Possible goal or destiny

10 The final outcome

9 Querent's hopes and ideals

1

2 Immediate influences

Present position of querent

4 Past influences

6 Future influences

8 Family and friends

3 Recent influences

7 Querent's negative feelings

Cards in Combination

If the Sun precedes Death, this means a triumphant end to something. When it follows the Tower, a sudden catastrophe will bring eventual benefit. When the Sun and the Two of Cups are together, two loving and positive people meld into a permanent relationship.

The WORLD

This positive card represents lessons learned, material and spiritual triumphs, a happy conclusion, or the end of a cycle in life.

LE MONDE

This is the material wish card, denoting spiritual as well as material success and reward. It also signifies joy, happiness, and sometimes long-distance travel across water and dreams coming true.

Suggested Reading

1 The querent deserves the inner contentment and joy that comes when, after hard work and many reversals, a long-held dream becomes a reality.

2 A wish is about to be granted or a pleasurable or important job that will bring success has been completed.

3 A lesson has been learned, a circle completed, or important work that will bring success has been finished.

4 You are now able to stand on your own two feet and accept responsibilities that will help you start a new life and career.

5 A wish will be granted, an ambition achieved, or you will reach your goal.

6 A dream you create will come true, provided you are not afraid of change and welcome responsibility.

7 Share your dreams and ambitions with others close to you and you will gain their support.

8 When discussing your views and ideas you must realize that others have thoughts on certain projects that are equally valid.

9 Wealth and success bring opportunities to travel across the world to interesting places. Do not be afraid to leave the familiar. You will be safe.

10 Indicates a dream come true, a major wish granted, a lesson learned, or the triumphant conclusion of a matter that brings you a long awaited happiness.

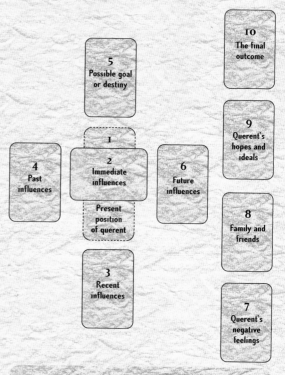

5 Possible goal or destiny

10 The final outcome

9 Querent's hopes and ideals

1

2 Immediate influences

Present position of querent

4 Past influences

6 Future influences

8 Family and friends

3 Recent influences

7 Querent's negative feelings

Cards in Combination

The World's spirituality and abstraction is negated by the proximity of Justice, the Hermit, and the Magician. If the Sun comes next to the World, an emotional experience will uplift and bring love, joy, and harmony. If the Hanged Man comes after the World, it means a triumph through a loving sacrifice, but if the World comes first a sacrifice could bring a sad parting.

JUDGMENT

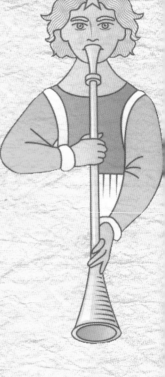

A very powerful and highly spiritual card representing the eternal spirit and a reincarnation or new lease of life.

LE JUGEMENT

This card symbolizes the end of one period in life and the beginning of another, rewards for past efforts, release, change and renewal, justified pride in achievement, a worthy life, and a mental awakening resulting in fame and success.

Suggested Reading

1 The querent is perceptive in many respects and wise, but can be too self-critical. Personal expression may have been sacrificed for the good of others.

2 Life is changing. Something is coming to an end but the past has taught you to face the future realistically with courage and honesty.

3 Work done well and a past that brings no guilt means you can hold your head up in pride.

4 Something has ended and old restrictions have been lifted. For the first time, you can think of yourself and adopt your chosen way of life.

5 Future success will come from using or restructuring creative efforts from the past to make an interesting new concept.

6 Symbolic of a mental awakening or sudden change that inspires new viewpoints and creative work, and brings fulfillment.

7 Self-healing comes from being honest with yourself and understanding that the cause of past failures may be due to your own weakness.

8 New ideas, a new location, or new work is needed to develop your talents and reach your goals in life. Do not be afraid of change.

9 The future is becoming clearer now that a lot of dead wood has been cleared away and you are seeing things as they really are.

10 The sun shines through the clouds, lighting up the path to be taken. All you need is determination and self-belief.

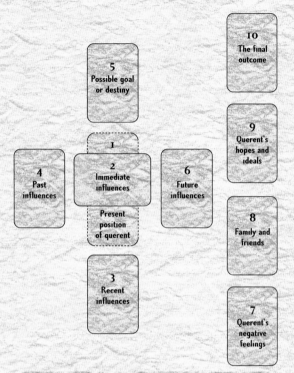

5
Possible goal or destiny

10
The final outcome

1

2
Immediate influences

Present position of querent

4
Past influences

6
Future influences

9
Querent's hopes and ideals

8
Family and friends

3
Recent influences

7
Querent's negative feelings

Cards in Combination

Followed by the Chariot, Judgment denotes fame and triumph. If the Chariot is reversed, sudden success will weaken the character and the triumph will only be temporary. If the Hermit follows Judgment, this means an inner spiritual triumph.

The Suits *The four suits—Cups, Wands (also known as Clubs, Batons, or Staves), Pentacles (also called Deniers or Discs), and Swords—are thought to derive from the four classes of society. The Cups represent the church; the Wands stand for farmers; the Pentacles symbolize moneymakers; and the Swords, fighting men. Some believe that the Cups might have represented the aristocracy; the Wands, landowners; the Pentacles, tradesmen; and the Swords, fighting men.*

The Suit of Cups

Water is changeable, can be both beautiful and dangerous, has different depths, and sometimes lies unseen and hidden deep below the earth. It is therefore not surprising that the Cups suit—linked to water— symbolizes the emotions and the subconscious. The Cups have always been linked with the church because they are portrayed in the oldest tarot decks as chalices. Yet, although given a spiritual dimension, these cards are linked more with worldly matters than spiritual conflict. The Cups are traditionally associated with the heart and its positive aspects, such as joy, dreams, romantic and spiritual love, worldly success and happiness stemming from luxury, the enjoyment of wealth, beauty, pleasure, fertility, and artistic creativity.

Two cards denoting romance, wealth, and creativity are the two of Cups and the nine of Cups. The first can describe a new love, a life-long friend, a happy reconciliation, and—depending upon surrounding cards—a joyous friend or lover. The nine of Cups is the wish card, which as well as symbolizing happiness in love and a legacy or a wish—possibly concerning money—also denotes creative success. The creative aspect of the Cups suit possibly derived from an association with the medieval church that kept many emotionally and religiously devoted scholars, artists, and scribes within its walls. This is demonstrated by the three of Cups, which symbolizes celebrating the completion of a creative project, while the seven of Cups denotes an offer or a dream that fuels creative ambitions.

Although the suit of Cups is more happy than sad and more positive than negative, it can also denote jealousy, hurt, pain, rejection, an overweening love of pleasure or luxury and vanity, and egotism and a preoccupation with self. The preponderance of Cups in a spread means problems have arisen through overemotionalism and the querent must discipline emotions to view life realistically.

Ace of Cups

Denotes a romantic meeting, or a new love affair, which—if near other love cards—will result in marriage, or, if near the Empress, can denote motherhood or creative inspiration. It also symbolizes joy in artistic endeavors, as well as spiritual nourishment, deep faith, happy company, and good news.

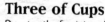

Two of Cups

Indicates a deep understanding of another that combines emotion with spirituality to create a permanent bond, a love affair, an engagement, a new partnership, or lasting friendship. It can suggest reconciliation after a parting, rivalry ended, a contract or agreement signed, a lovely surprise, and limited support or money given.

Three of Cups

Denotes the feminine element in nature bringing emotional growth, love, and fulfillment in a marriage or relationship. Sensitivity to others and a capacity for giving means that love and friendship will light the querent's future. Could also signify a victorious conclusion to a matter and creative ability bringing joyous rewards.

Four of Cups

Suggests that discontent with the querent's present life will lead to self-examination and a search for a new direction in life or a change of career. It can also mean that meddling, jealousy, or hostility from others could ruin a budding romance or friendship and advises listening to the inner voice.

Five of Cups

Symbolic of something finished
and something new beginning.
New paths are about to be explored
or a new life is about to start.
May also denote an inheritance,
regrets after loss, a love affair
finished, or past behavior or a
mistake made, with the warning
that one's inner voice and
spiritual needs must never
be ignored.

Six of Cups

Indicates that past efforts or
contacts will now bring benefits.
It points to something that had
its beginnings in the past, such as
a love affair, a long-held ambition,
or an old friend who is about to
reappear. The results of past actions
may now influence the present
and this card warns you
not to live in the past.

Seven of Cups

Denotes an unexpected and exceptional
offer requiring wisdom to make the right
choice in order to see a dream fulfilled.
It also symbolizes mystical experiences,
as well as mental ability and creative
inspiration, that could bring surprising
rewards, but with a warning that
the querent could be become a
"Jack of all trades, master of none."

Eight of Cups

Expresses a deep spiritual change brought about by suffering or disillusionment. It can signify a new maturity through suffering, forgetting the past and seeking new paths in life, new activities that bring much happiness, leaving a place or a situation behind, and meeting new, genuine friends of an artistic and spiritual nature.

Nine of Cups

Strong and positive, the "wish card" denotes both material and emotional security, the complete fulfillment of one major wish or desire in life. This card also symbolizes generosity, kindliness, good health, intuitive awareness, and good luck, but with a warning that overindulgence or contentment in the pleasures of life could undermine artistic endeavors or commitments.

Ten of Cups

Implies deep and lasting spiritual peace and happiness, honor and lasting success, fame, prestige, and publicity, work in a public sphere, the love of friends, and a journey that has a happy ending. It can also pertain to buying or selling, and successful legal matters related to property and residence.

Knave of Cups

Describes an artistic, meditative, and loyal young person of either sex, under 21, who can deceive through being overimaginative or overemotional. This card also signifies news or a message, new business methods, the birth of a child, or a change that alters and improves the future.

VALET DE COUPE

Knight of Cups

Symbolizes a man between 21 and 35, high-principled—except possibly in emotional matters — intelligent, but somewhat egotistical, and romantic, but sometimes devious. Can indicate a lover, rival, friend, or a fated relationship that teaches a lesson. May also signify the bearer of a message, an invitation, a proposition, or a pleasant visit.

CAVALIER DE COUPE

Queen of Cups

Symbolic of the beloved wife or mistress. Romantic, sensitive, intuitive, and slightly fey, artistically gifted, a good mixer, and a kind of loving idealist, she practices what she preaches. This card can indicate new romance or new horizons, but if badly aspected can mean overdominance, moodiness, self-deception, and false romanticism.

REYNE DE COUPE

King of Cups

A worldly, powerful man of ideas, over 35, from any walk of life, but often a professional connected with law, education, medicine, or religion. Warmhearted and sympathetic, he tends to hide emotion. Both sensitive and creative, he can give reliable advice and help, but can be crafty and often puts himself first.

ROY DE COUPE

The Suit of Wands

In early tarot packs, this suit was also known as Clubs, Batons, or Staves. All were depicted as thick, leafy branches of a tree signifying growth, flowering, and renewal, and were believed to represent landowners or farmers.

Primarily this suit symbolizes strength, energy, commercial activity, growth, and expansion that can include deep-sea travel and foreign countries.

Wands are also connected with fire, which in ancient times was believed to emanate from nothing and transform anything it touched, yet remain unaltered itself. It was linked with the fire of creative imagination, which transforms reality and gives it a deeper meaning, thus the suit of Wands also describes the use of creative talent and the tests, challenges, and hurdles that an artist has to meet in order to retain his or her integrity.

Wands also denote important and lasting values, such as emotional and material security, serenity, creativity, inner development, inner security and stability.

A key quality of this suit is strength in adversity, which results in the attainment of security after hard work, trials, and struggle. The nine of Wands is the strongest card in the Minor Arcana, indicating personal and economic stability, and security coming after hard work and prolonged effort. When there are a large number of Wands in a spread, you may be sure that the querent has creative talents and has worked hard and endured trials that have helped develop self-honesty and spirituality.

Ace of Wands

Symbolic of new beginnings, the renewal of energies, or a new foundation that brings success and satisfaction.

This card also signifies innovation, artistic inspiration bringing a new cycle of creative activity, new wisdom or knowledge, and a dissatisfaction with present circumstances or attitudes; the founding of a fortune or family.

Two of Wands

Denotes high motives, tolerance, justice, intellectual work, help from people in authority, consistent effort, overcoming obstacles, authority, and success won through strength and vision. Courage, willpower, and initiative have led the querent to achieve maturity, future happiness, and lasting success.

Three of Wands

Significant of the artist or inventor. With powerful convictions and powers of expression, original or inspirational work brings recognition and success. This card also symbolizes help from a powerful associate, artistic or creative ideas becoming reality, a partnership bringing wealth and renown, a business enterprise, and a warning against carelessness.

Four of Wands

Represents the gifted and successful inventor or designer, combining the world of ideas with the beauty of perfected work. It can mean a pause in activities or a peaceful period away from the demands of everyday life, as well as harmony, romance, close family ties, and gathering in the harvest after long, hard labor.

Five of Wands

Denotes the triumph of love over obstacles, or a determined struggle that overcomes material adversity—but with the warning that mental ability is needed to triumph, then a change for the better will follow. Badly aspected, the five of Wands signifies carelessness in legal matters or bitterness through unfulfilled desires.

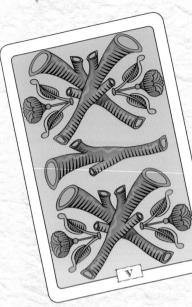

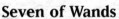

Six of Wands

The career card of the Minor Arcana, the six of Wands denotes a triumphant achievement in one's career, wonderful news, the fulfillment of ambitions, victory in a difficult situation, the solution to a major problem, success after a struggle, diplomacy, overcoming opposition, public acclaim, and satisfaction, but also triumph soured by others' envy.

Seven of Wands

Known as the teacher's card, the seven of Wands symbolizes the dissemination of knowledge, lecturing, and writing. It also denotes success achieved by inner strength and determination, sustained effort and courage needed to defeat opposition, and a successful change in profession. Badly aspected, it reveals envy from others, the need for competitiveness, and failure due to indecision.

Eight of Wands

Symbolic of movement, speed, haste
in travel, taking a sudden journey,
usually by air, the end of a quiet
period or of a delay, sudden
changes which spell progress
in life, unexpected news that
arrives suddenly, overseas
connections, and the
sudden arrows of love.
Time to be trying something new.

Nine of Wands

The strength card of the Minor
Arcana denotes the lasting triumph
through strength and integrity that
brings victory after a final challenge.
It also symbolizes success or
expansion in the artistic or
professional fields, sound advice
given or taken, balanced judgment,
courage in defense, strength in
reserve, and a trusting nature.

Ten of Wands

Problems solved. Represents
burdens soon to be lifted; narrow-
minded or fixed ideas must go to
make progress in a new direction.
The card symbolizes consolidation,
big business, new contracts or
ventures, an overseas trip or a
journey to a strange place. Badly
aspected, it means fear of risk
and an unrealistic opinion of
one's abilities.

Knave of Wands

Indicates a spiritual and adaptable young person, under 21, male or female, with creative potential but still looking for a direction in life. Also a messenger or a postman with news from a loved one, or with pleasing news concerning finances. It also denotes creative inspiration that needs developing and the fear of domination.

VALET DE BATON

CAVALIER DE BATON

Knight of Wands

Denotes a charming, lovable man between 21 and 35. A volatile personality who likes change and travel. This card signifies a change of residence, a departure or flight, distant travel, or a stable sense in money matters. Badly aspected it can represent a jealous lover, rivalry, interference in business, or a lack of energy.

Queen of Wands

Symbolic of an intuitive, tolerant, protective woman, generous, independent, strongwilled, determined, and confident. A home and country lover, often artistic or creative, who makes a good friend, but when badly aspected is dominating, bitter, judgmental, and narrow-minded. It can also imply successful new creative or business ventures.

REYNE DE BATON

King of Wands

Symbolic of an honest, generous, and courageous man, over 35. A born leader, enthusiastic and intelligent, who could be successful in most financial, professional, or creative fields. He gives wise impartial advice and sympathy. This card also denotes an unexpected inheritance or successful business. When badly aspected, this King can be power hungry.

ROY DE BATON

The suit of Pentacles, or Deniers, corresponds with our material existence. These cards cover all aspects of finance, such as gains and losses through commercial activities, the risks and challenges of new commercial ventures, and sometimes litigation connected with financial concerns. It also concerns the commencement and award of stability and financial security, and the worth we place on our own achievements.

The Suit of Pentacles

Pentacles can signify training in commercial, scientific, and creative fields resulting in status, a well-paid living, and monetary rewards. Professions such as financial management, teaching, chemistry, medicine, journalism, and commercial art are particularly aligned to the Pentacles suit. These cards can imply generous help from wealthy, powerful people, inheritance, and the founding of a family fortune. On the negative side, they may also denote a bleak period of worry and isolation caused by unemployment, disappointment in money or career, and meanness verging on miserliness. Pentacles tell us that money is the root of all evil and that misusing it— by either worshipping or despising it—brings extreme suffering and spiritual poverty.

In a spread where kindly, emotional Cups predominate alongside Pentacles, the querent cares for others or is interested in healing or drama. If the older male court cards from the Swords suit, the Emperor, or Justice are close to the same cards, it can indicate a career in politics.

Ace of Pentacles

Signifies the appreciation of physical beauty, sensuousness, materialism, love of possessions, pride in the ability to succeed, prosperity, gold, luxury, gifts, legacies, stoicism, endurance, security built on a firm foundation, and an enterprise about to begin that will bring solid financial benefit. If badly aspected, it is symbolic of greed or overconfidence.

Two of Pentacles

Denotes imminent change, harmony in the midst of change, skillful manipulation during sudden domestic or financial changes, new moves to make, or success in one direction. This card indicates that the use of one talent will bring rewards, and also symbolizes literary ability and a journey or a move to a new home or country. Badly aspected, the two of Pentacles advises that emotional instability will cause problems.

Three of Pentacles

The card of professionalism and craftsmanship, the three of Pentacles explains that hard work, training, and consistent effort bring success and recognition in work or a career. This card denotes skill in a trade, artistic ability that brings financial rewards and honor, help, cooperation from others, and the time for successful expansion in business. If badly aspected, expect loss through lack of direction.

Four of Pentacles

This card of finance denotes both material and financial stability, also the love of possession and acquisitiveness, financial concerns with both benefits and problems, a legacy or inheritance, and the establishment of a commercial firm or business. If badly aspected, this card signifies meanness with money, business problems, and low self-esteem.

Five of Pentacles

Emotions that rule the intellect bring loss of judgment, sorrow or disappointment, loss of work or position, loss of a home or lover, and enforced restrictions and spiritual loneliness. Lasting friendships will be made with those in similar circumstances. When near positive cards, it means faith in oneself is regained and a new start is made.

Six of Pentacles

This entertainment or theatrical card denotes work such as acting, singing, dancing, or lecturing, but is also a strongly spiritual card, symbolizing help from above, help from a good, generous person, sympathy, kindness, charity, just rewards, or finances becoming stable. When badly aspected, it expresses the inability to give of oneself.

Seven of Pentacles

This card tells us that procrastination is the thief of time. Consistent work is needed to bring past efforts to a successful completion. It can indicate that something is changing, or that results from the past are about to bear fruit. Also symbolic of a new love and money, in the form of a successful barter or a loan, although possibly delayed.

Eight of Pentacles

The talent and energy card denotes changes coming from turning a recently discovered or developed skill into a profession, money earned in the future through talents and skills being developed at present, possible future employment in a new skilled field, or labor rewarded. When badly aspected, this card symbolizes failure through laziness.

Nine of Pentacles

Signifies the independence and individuality of a uniquely talented person who must learn that inner peace and satisfaction come through self-knowledge. Also symbolizes material wealth or substantial income earned by sound administration and consistent effort. The successful completion of a project brings reward or the solution to a problem.

Ten of Pentacles

Denotes material, creative, and spiritual wealth generously shared with others and rewards from creative achievements. Pertaining to house and family, the ten of Pentacles symbolizes a reverence for history, establishing new traditions, a settled way of life, bloodties, inheritance, dowries, legacies, purchase, or sale. If badly aspected, this card indicates that restrictive ties become a burden.

Knave of Pentacles

Symbolic of a person under 21, of either sex,
with a respect for scholarship, new ideas, and
opinions, the person is diligent and ambitious
but often materialistic and mean with money.
It also denotes a letter containing money
or a message bringing good news. If
badly aspected, this card
describes wasted talent,
unrealistic ambitions,
or intellectual snobbery.

VALET DE DENIERS

CAVALIER DE DENIERS

Knight of Pentacles

Denotes a young man under 35,
honorable, traditional, determined,
and materialistic, with a love of nature
and animals. Also indicative of a new
acquaintance or an indiscreet flirtation.
It also expresses the patience needed
to finish boring and laborious work
or the beginning and end of a matter.
Badly aspected, expect errors through
timidity or stagnation.

Queen of Pentacles

Describes a practical, industrious, independent woman, delighting in the good things of life, but giving generously to people she likes and respects. Sometimes financially independent, socially adept, and interested in creative arts, she carries the connotation of money and responsibility in wealth. Badly aspected, she is insecure, untrusting, and materialistic.

REYNE DE DENIERS

King of Pentacles

Indicates a stable, patient man, over 35, with a flair for mathematics, although often uneducated and inarticulate. He possesses a deliberate turn of mind and intuitive wisdom, and is loyally protective of friends. A good parent but a bad enemy, he is often connected with financial matters, and when badly aspected is easy to bribe.

ROY DE DENIERS

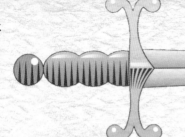

The Suit of Swords

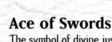

The symbol of the two-edged sword caused some early scholars to ignore the deeper spiritual meanings of this suit, and to declare that Swords are strongly negative and signify physical aggression, loss, pain, and destruction. Being two-edged, swords have both positive and negative meanings, all of which help to form the mind and character. The negative cards denote emotional and spiritual development through sacrifice, loss, loneliness of spirit, accepting defeat, enduring sorrow, wounding words, quarrels, conflicts, harsh judgments, separations, and challenges and upheavals requiring great strength and faith to overcome. They bring maturity because we see things as they are and not as we want them to be.

The Swords suit also includes such positive meanings as courage, intellectual and spiritual strength, boldness, hope, solitude, meditation, peace in the midst of strife, and a removal to a new home, starting life in a new direction, or a journey into consciousness. The ace of Swords is not an unfortunate card, although it can symbolize—depending on the cards surrounding it— the sword of Damocles about to descend or the symbol of divine justice. It can also indicate illness, conquest, power, and strength in adversity, or something inevitable about to begin that cannot be stopped. The predominance of Swords in any spread means that— unless the High Priestess, the Hierophant, the Hermit, or the Fool are present—the querent is dominated by the physical aspects of life and faces future aggression and conflict.

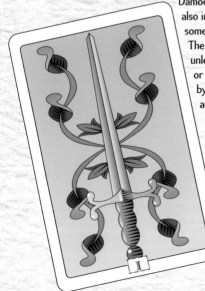

Ace of Swords

The symbol of divine justice reveals that you reap what you sow. This card signifies conquest, a sense of the inevitable, and a strong force for good or ill. Something that cannot be stopped is likely to change the querent's entire perspective on life. The ace of Swords symbolizes strength in adversity and triumph over obstacles. If badly aspected, disappointment will come, but will be followed by a victory.

Two of Swords

The card of balanced forces or stalemate. The two of Swords denotes a sense of equilibrium, good coming out of evil, and help and friendship in adversity. It tells us that making a difficult choice will bring spiritual peace and satisfaction. Badly aspected, it can suggest you will make the wrong choice through self-deception, indecision, and living in the past.

Three of Swords

This card signifies permanent or temporary separation, a marital breakup, severing a partnership, disruption, upheaval, pain followed by healing, or the sense that the ground is clearing for something better. Badly aspected, it is symbolic of civil strife and dwelling on old hurts.

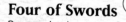

Four of Swords

Peace and order comes after struggle or chaos. This card also denotes administration in legal matters—in a civic sense and personally—hospitalization, convalescence, and a voluntary retreat after a testing time in order to think things through. Badly aspected, this card indicates feelings of isolation, postponing a decision, and the need to use diplomacy.

Five of Swords

Accept the inevitable, recognize false
pride, acknowledge your limitations,
face defeat courageously, learn to build
on secure foundations, choose a new
direction in order to move onward and
upward. This card may indicate a narrow
escape from physical danger or a threat
averted. If this card is badly aspected,
understand that fear and insecure
foundations bring defeat
and humiliation.

Six of Swords

This card of flight or travel denotes change
to a better environment or a change of work,
success after anxiety, obstacles removed
after a stressful period, the end of a difficult
time, or good news brought by
an overseas visitor. It tells us
that risk brings reward. If the
card is badly aspected, be patient,
time will solve a problem.

Seven of Swords

Explains that foresight, cunning,
prudence, and evasion are all needed
to thwart an enemy, solve a problem,
or sidestep an obstacle to achieve
success or gain an objective. Use brain
rather than brawn. Aggressive tactics
bring disaster. Greed can affect
principles. Badly aspected, plans
have altered or negative
thinking about mistakes
blocks progress.

Eight of Swords

Restrictions will soon be lifted and bonds broken, but self-deception, hypocrisy, negativity, and lack of confidence cause indecision. Self-honesty, confidence, and attention to detail are needed to change the status quo and avoid criticism from others. Favorably aspected, it signifies hurts healed, progress made, and new self-confidence.

Nine of Swords

Symbolic of patient suffering borne with courage and fortitude; illness, isolation, loss, the news of a death or an accident brings sadness; a difficult choice entailing sacrifice, self-punishment, and a sense of despair. Favorably aspected, it signifies shedding the past, beginning a new, productive, active existence —time heals all wounds.

Ten of Swords

Denotes the lowest point in the national economy, the lowest ebb of human affairs, and a self-honesty that sees something clearly for the first time for what it really is, not what it seems to be. Badly aspected, the card signifies misfortune and pain. Favorably aspected, it indicates self-acceptance, the end of spiritual darkness, and rebirth.

Knave of Swords

Symbolic of a young person under 21 of either sex. Possibly has inner conflict from injustice during childhood, he or she is independent, with unpredictable moods, can act mischievously, be frivolous, manipulative, devious, and cruel. Also a diplomatic messenger who negotiates business matters or an unscrupulous business rival or spy.

VALET D'ÉPÉE

Knight of Swords

This card represents a career-minded man betweeen 21 and 35. At his best in a difficult situation, he is a courageous fighter, skilled in defense, impetuous, passionate, and sometimes ruthless. The card also symbolizes a foreigner, a foreign country, or a conflict to be faced. If close cards mean illness, he could represent a surgeon.

CAVALIER D'ÉPÉE

REYNE D'ÉPÉE

Queen of Swords

The widow's card denotes a self-reliant, intelligent, strong, and cautious woman, often intolerant and spiteful, who makes a good friend but a bad enemy. Carrying the connotation of sadness and privation, this card also denotes a struggle between spiritual and material values, and a foreign woman or nation.

King of Swords

An authoritative man over 35, he is a professional with moral convictions, an intellectual with an innovative mind, a lawyer or adviser, an officer, or a high government official. This card also denotes a foreign man or nation. Badly aspected, he is a severe critic and can be cruel, violent, and vengeful.

ROY D'ÉPÉE

INDEX & CREDITS

Quarto would like to acknowledge and thank the following for providing pictures used in this book:

Illustrations from the Visconti-Sforza, Dragon and Morgan-Greer Tarot decks reproduced by permission of U.S. Games Systems, Inc., Stamford, CT 06902 USA. Copyrights © 1975, 1996, 1993 by U.S. Games Systems, Inc. Further reproduction prohibited. Swiss IJJ Tarot © 1970 reproduced by permission of U.S. Games Systems, Inc. and AGMuller, Neuhausen and Rheinfall, Switzerland. *Illustrations from the Lord of the Rings Tarot Deck* reproduced by permission of U.S. Games Systems, Inc., Stamford, CT under license of Tolkien Enterprises, a

division of The Saul Zaentz Company, Berkeley, CA. Copyright © 1997 by Tolkien Enterprises. Further reproduction prohibited. *Illustrations from the Crowley Thoth Tarot decks* reproduced by permission of Ordo Templi Orientis, Copyright © Ordo Templi Orientis 1944, 2001. *Photograph on page 5:* Christie's Images. All other images are the copyright of Quarto. While every effort has been made to acknowledge copyright holders, we would like to apologize should there have been any omissions.